CONTENTS

The Manning brothers' unique position as both brothers and rivals has made them two of the most familiar faces in the United States, and sporting superstars worldwide.

There cannot be many people in the United States who do not know the story of Peyton and Eli Manning. Predicted to become National Football League (NFL) superstars from an early age, the brothers have gone on to become two of the most successful quarterbacks of all time.

In the history of football, no other players can match the Mannings' extraordinary records. It is unusual for two brothers to both play in the NFL, let alone both excel at their chosen sport. The Manning brothers have done just that, each winning at least one Super Bowl, picking up Most Valuable Player awards along the way, as well.

It's not just the brothers' sporting excellence that has made them famous. They have also devoted considerable time and money to good causes. Few athletes have done more for charities, or the communities in which they live, than Peyton and Eli. They are modern sports legends.

CHAPTER 1

THE MANNING BROTHERS' STORY

Archie Manning always expected his sons Peyton (born March 24, 1976, in New Orleans, Louisiana) and Eli (born January 3, 1981, in New Orleans, Louisiana) to be good football players. Archie had once enjoyed a successful professional career as an NFL quarterback himself, and always dreamed that his sons would follow in his footsteps. From an early age, Eli and Peyton showed signs of developing into great quarterbacks. By the time he left high school in 1993, Peyton was widely regarded as a football star in the making. He led the football team of Isidore Newman School in

Peyton earns millions each year from his football career and his numerous sponsorship deals and commercials.

New Orleans for three years, helping the team achieve an astonishing win-loss record of 34–5.

At high school, Peyton's younger brother, Eli, did not achieve quite the same football feats as his older sibling. However, he was still one of the outstanding high school quarterbacks in the country. Peyton knew it, too. When he left Isidore Newman School in 1993, Peyton wrote the following words about Eli in his yearbook: "Watch out, world, he's the best one!"

STAR STATS

As a high school football player, Peyton Manning won a number of awards. In his final year at school in 1993, he was named Gatorade Circle of Champions National Player of the Year and Columbus (Ohio) Touchdown Club National Offensive Player of the Year.

FROM ROOKIE TO MVP

By the time he graduated from the University of Tennessee, Peyton Manning had been marked out as a future NFL superstar. The player held an amazing record with his college football team, the Tennessee Volunteers. Of the 45 games Peyton started, the Volunteers won an incredible 39, losing only six.

When he joined the Indianapolis Colts, Peyton's contribution to the team was significant. In less than five years, Peyton transformed them from also-rans to playoff contenders.

In early 1998, Peyton put himself forward for the annual NFL Draft, in which teams sign the best college football talent. As predicted, Peyton was the first pick, and was chosen by the Indianapolis Colts. Six years later, in 2004, brother Eli also became the first pick in the NFL Draft, completing a rare double-first-pick for the Manning boys.

Peyton soon made his mark with the Colts. In his first season, he set four NFL rookie records, including the most touchdown passes in a season. So great was Peyton's contribution to the Colts that, in both 2003 and 2004, he was named Associated Press (AP) NFL Most Valuable Player (MVP).

STAR STATS

By the time he left college, Peyton Manning had become the University of Tennessee Volunteers' all-time leading passer, with 11,201 yards (10,242 m) and 89 touchdowns.

SUPER BOWL STARS

Football fans love players who break records, produce moments of magic, and turn a losing team into a championship winner. Yet, to be considered true all-time greats, quarterbacks must make their mark in the biggest game of all—the Super Bowl.

Achieving success in the Super Bowl can turn football greats into sporting immortals. By this measure, the Manning brothers are football legends. Their remarkable Super Bowl record began in February 2007, when Peyton was named Super Bowl Most Valuable Player after leading the Indianapolis Colts to a 29–17 win over the Chicago Bears.

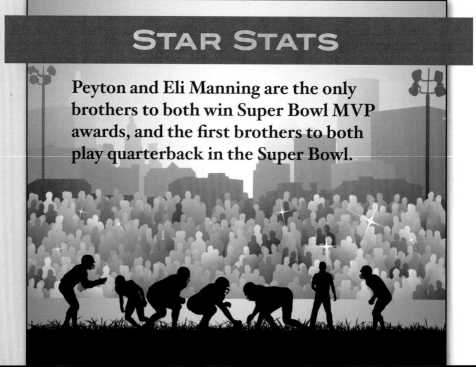

STAR STATS

Peyton and Eli Manning are the only brothers to both win Super Bowl MVP awards, and the first brothers to both play quarterback in the Super Bowl.

Eli Manning has twice won the Super Bowl, leading the New York Giants to wins over the New England Patriots in 2008 and 2012.

A year later, Eli also got his chance to play on the Super Bowl stage. In an outstanding performance that won him the Super Bowl MVP award, Eli became the first quarterback to throw two touchdown passes in the final quarter. Eli's skills helped his New York Giants beat the game's favorites, the New England Patriots, 17–14.

In February 2012, Eli's New York Giants once more faced the New England Patriots in Super Bowl XLVI—and won once again.

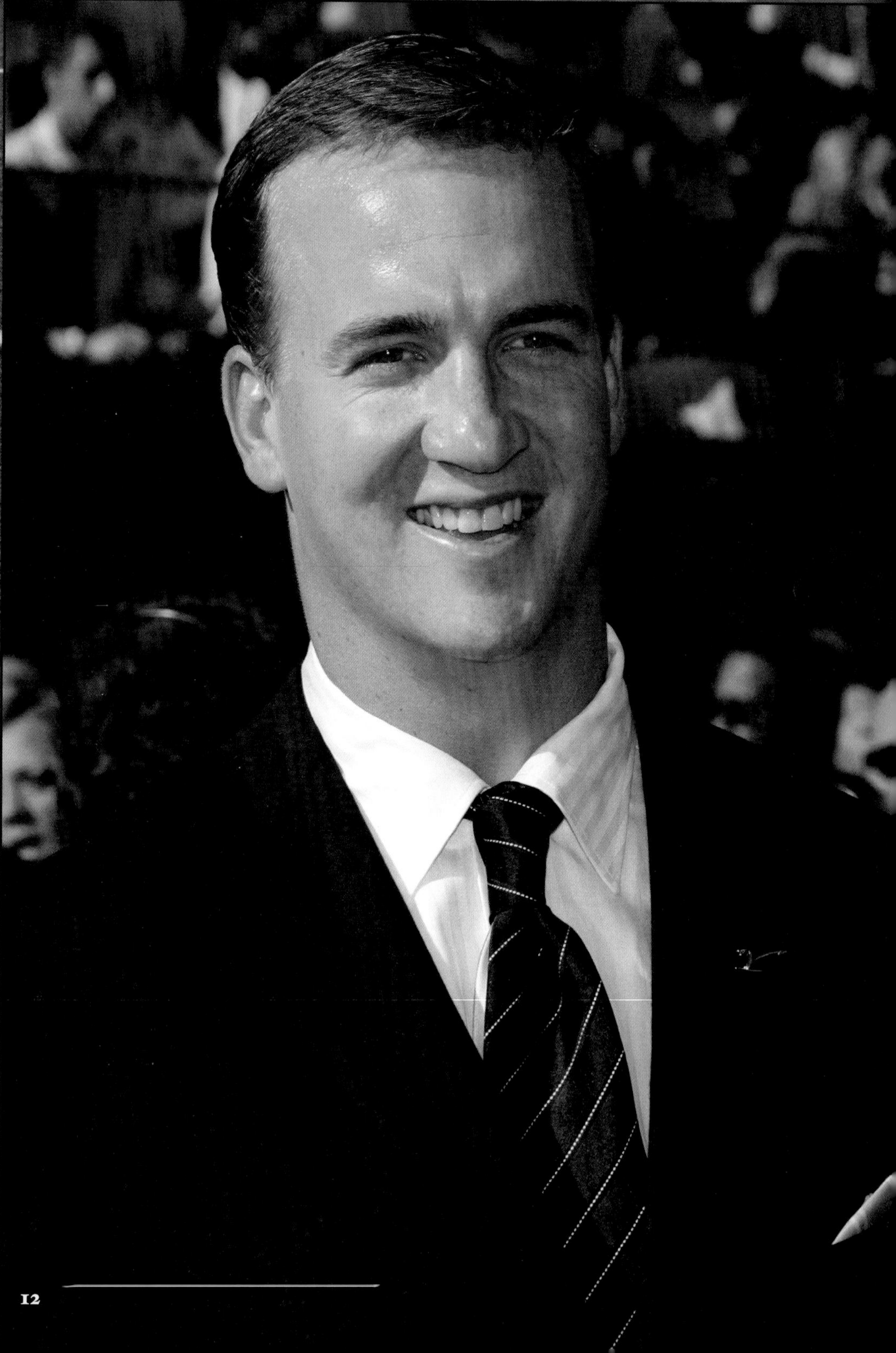

Stars Off the Field

The Manning brothers' record-breaking careers and Super Bowl wins have made them stars. Many football players are famous, but few are quite as well known and well loved as Peyton and Eli Manning.

It's not just the brothers' performances that make them two of the NFL's most marketable players. Both married their college sweethearts, are committed fathers, and are widely thought of as great role models. The brothers' great personal qualities make them appealing to fans and sponsors alike. Between them, Peyton and Eli have appeared on commercials for Kraft, Reebok, Citizen Watch, Toyota, Samsung, and DirecTV.

Eli and Peyton have also appeared in a number of popular television shows. Both have hosted the world-famous comedy show *Saturday Night Live*, Peyton in 2007, and Eli in 2012. Together with elder brother Cooper, the brothers were even featured in a 2009 episode of *The Simpsons*.

The popular Manning brothers are invited to numerous red carpet events. Here, Peyton Manning arrives at a recent Excellence in Sports Performance Yearly (ESPY) Awards in Hollywood.

More than Football Players

The Manning brothers' model family lives and sporting greatness make them outstanding role models. Throughout their careers, the brothers have also given a huge amount of time, and a sizeable amount of their multimillion-dollar fortunes, to helping good causes.

Peyton and Eli have always had a passion for helping those less fortunate than themselves. They realize that they are very lucky to be able to earn vast sums of money doing what they love best—football. The brothers are determined to use their wealth, and their high profile, to improve the lives of others less fortunate than themselves.

To ensure he would be able to make a significant contribution to society, Peyton established his own charity, the PeyBack Foundation. Eli is also a significant contributor to charitable causes. Since 2007, Eli has hosted the largest charity golf event in Westchester County, New York, in aid of the Guiding Eyes for the Blind dog school. He was also inspired to take part by a blind family friend, Patrick Brown Jr. The tournament raises more than half a million dollars each year.

Eli Manning gives instructions to his Giants players ahead of a game against the Atlanta Falcons in December 2012. Eli and Peyton are now almost as famous for their work for good causes as for their outstanding football performances.

STAR STATS

Eli Manning currently holds five NFL records, including most fourth quarter touchdown passes in a season (15 in 2011), and most "road" wins in a single season by a starting quarterback (10).

15

In 1999, just one year into his professional football career, Peyton Manning decided to give something back to his community and launched the PeyBack Foundation.

The foundation's goal is simple—to give disadvantaged children a head start in life by working with charities and organizations that promote healthy lifestyles, teach leadership skills, and encourage learning. On his website,

Peyton Manning is famous for his involvement with his local communities. Here, he heads up the 500 Festival Parade of Indy cars in Indianapolis, Ind.

Peyton explains his goals for the PeyBack Foundation: "Children need opportunities through which they can grow and learn... From the outset, we have strived to match up the dollars we can provide with children in need."

The PeyBack Foundation makes a difference not only by running its own programs and health campaigns, but also through donating money to charities for disadvantaged children.

STAR STATS

The PeyBack Foundation works exclusively in four states with which Peyton has links. The states are:
- Louisiana, where Peyton was born.
- Tennessee, where the football player went to college.
- Indiana, where Peyton spent most of his career playing for the Colts.
- Colorado, where Peyton plays for the Denver Broncos.

DIGGING DEEP

Peyton Manning is determined to ensure that the PeyBack Foundation provides as much funding to charitable causes as possible. Therefore, the funds the foundation aims to raise each year are sizeable.

Peyton himself digs deep, funding a large portion of the charity from his own career earnings with the Colts and the Denver Broncos. The charity regularly receives funding from the NFL Charities Grant,

In 2013, at the Legends For Charity dinner in honor of Archie Manning, Peyton and Eli describe how their father inspired their football careers and charity work.

and in 2012 alone was awarded over $20,000. The PeyBack Foundation also accepts donations from private individuals, from $50 to many thousands of dollars.

To raise more funds, every year since 2003, Peyton has hosted a bowling tournament called the PeyBack Bowl. The star-studded event is open only to people who donate money to the foundation, and gives fans a chance to bowl alongside football players and famous celebrities. As of 2013, the PeyBack Bowl has raised more than $2.3 million for the PeyBack Foundation.

STAR STATS

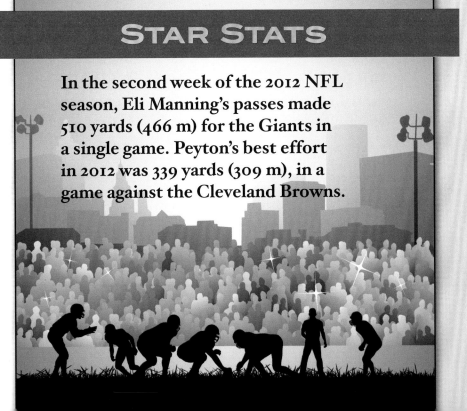

In the second week of the 2012 NFL season, Eli Manning's passes made 510 yards (466 m) for the Giants in a single game. Peyton's best effort in 2012 was 339 yards (309 m), in a game against the Cleveland Browns.

GIVING BACK

Every year, the PeyBack Foundation gives grants to charities working with children. Since it was set up in 1999, the foundation has helped change the lives of hundreds of thousands of underprivileged children.

To obtain PeyBack Foundation funds, charities must write to the foundation and apply for a grant of up to $10,000. The charities must explain exactly how the money will be used to help children, whether that is by helping them to read, funding after-school classes to

STAR STATS

In 2011, Peyton Manning's season suffered a setback when the footballer injured his neck and back. The next season, Peyton left the Indianapolis Colts and joined the Denver Broncos. He was an instant success and won the NFL's Comeback Player of the Year Award in 2012.

In 2010, Eli traded on the New York Stock Exchange to raise money for the BGC finance company's BGC Charity Day. The event is held every year to commemorate the lives of the 658 employees the company lost in the 9/11 attacks.

keep kids off the streets, or by teaching children new skills.

In 2012 alone, the PeyBack Foundation paid over $500,000 in grants to charities in Tennessee, Louisiana, and Indiana. Eighty-eight charities benefited from PeyBack Foundation cash. Recipients included Girl Scout groups, local community centers, Christian charities, youth theaters, YMCA centers, holiday camps for inner-city kids, the Salvation Army, and the American Red Cross. Money was also awarded to children's homes, after-school music clubs, and charities that offer help to families in need.

Help for the Holidays

The holiday season is an important time of year for all children. However, many children across the United States do not experience the fun, presents, and activities that other, more fortunate, children associate with the holidays. To make sure that disadvantaged children enjoy the holidays, Peyton Manning sees that a portion of the PeyBack Foundation's annual funds is held back to pay for a special program of events for children around Thanksgiving and Christmas.

Each year, Peyton Manning hosts the PeyBack Holiday Celebration. This is a series of "holiday happenings" for children and their families. Events vary from paying for turkey meals for children attending Boys and Girls Clubs, to Peyton himself distributing heating vouchers and groceries to the needy. Whatever the contribution, the aim is to spread some holiday cheer among those who need it most.

Since 2008, Peyton has hosted special holiday parties at the Louisiana Children's Museum. In 2012, the party was for students of Lake Pontchartrain Elementary School in Louisiana, who had seen their school buildings badly damaged by Hurricane Isaac four months earlier. Each schoolchild received a "goody bag" that contained a book, a healthy lunch, and a warm, orange fleece blanket. As of 2012, more than 2,500 children have enjoyed a fun-filled day at the museum.

Schoolchildren from Lake Pontchartrain Elementary School enjoyed a holiday party that would have been impossible were it not for the PeyBack Foundation.

23

AWARDING OTHERS

The PeyBack Foundation's contribution to children across the United States is significant. Each year, millions of dollars are raised through the foundation's donations to charity or fundraising work. Despite his already powerful contribution, Peyton Manning continually wants to do more. To raise additional funds, the sports star now hosts a yearly award for people involved in professional football who are also making a difference in their community. The award is called the PeyBack Award.

The recipient of the PeyBack Award is a person chosen by Peyton himself, and is often someone from the world of professional football who "exhibits character, integrity, and honor." Like Peyton, the person has also usually given back to both the game and his or her community. Each winner receives a check for $5,000, which is then given to a charity of the winner's choice.

Previous winners of the prestigious award include Pro Football Hall of Fame members Gale Sayers, Marshall Faulk, Derrick Brooks, Roger Staubach, Dan Marino, and Jim Kelly.

Kurt Warner's First Things First Foundation improves the lives of thousands of families through outreach programs, trips, and fundraising events.

In 2010, the PeyBack Award was presented to recently retired quarterback and former Super Bowl MVP Kurt Warner, in recognition of his outstanding contribution to people in need in his community through his charity, the First Things First Foundation.

CHAPTER 3

LEADING BY EXAMPLE

Many charitable sportspeople make a difference in their communities by donating money to good causes, and by using their fame to raise awareness of people experiencing hardship. Peyton and Eli Manning use their high-profile status and standing in the sports community to boost the profile of charities, causes, and organizations they care about. Although charities must raise money, they also must raise awareness of their fundraising efforts. By asking celebrities and famous sports stars to back

Here, Peyton Manning demonstrates his football skills by playing a superb action pass with running back Mike Hart against the Jacksonville Jaguars.

their campaigns or help with their programs, Eli and Peyton ensure great coverage of their causes, and thereby drive up public donations to the charities.

Peyton and Eli Manning are well known for giving their time freely to charities and good causes. Both have been involved in raising money for local children's hospitals, and aim to inspire young football players by giving them hints, tips, and coaching clinics. They also regularly visit sick children, and have been known to help aid workers following terrible national disasters, such as 2005's Hurricane Katrina.

STAR STATS

By June 2013, Eli Manning had made 146 consecutive starts as quarterback for the New York Giants. Only two other quarterbacks in NFL history, brother Peyton (227) and Brett Favre (321), have made more consecutive starts.

PLAY LIKE PEYTON

With three NFL quarterbacks in the family, it's no surprise that the Mannings are eager to inspire children to become potentially sensational football players. Every summer, Peyton, Eli, and their father, Archie, coach children at the Manning Passing Academy. This is a series of summer camps for enthusiastic high school football players.

The summer camps are not completely free of charge, and placement is limited. This means that some children who apply are not accepted, and others do not have the means by which to apply. In order to address the issue, Peyton has used the PeyBack Foundation to launch another football initiative that doesn't cost applicants a dime—the PeyBack Classic.

The PeyBack Classic is a competition that gives Indianapolis public high school football teams the chance to play at the home of the local professional football team, the Colts. Between 2000 and 2007, that meant playing at the RCA Dome. Since then, the PeyBack Classic has been held at the new home of the Colts, the Lucas Oil Stadium.

By 2013, more than 30 different high school teams from Indianapolis had taken part in the PeyBack Classic. Year after year, the charitable competition continues to be one of the most popular events on the local sports calendar.

Peyton Manning showing rookie football players how to play to Super Bowl standard at the Manning Passing Academy in Thibodaux, Louisiana.

ACTION MANNINGS

In times of national emergency or devastating natural disasters, the United States pulls together to help those in need. This can take the form of donating money, helping to raise awareness of a disaster and its outcome, or even helping out on the ground. Over the years, Peyton and Eli Manning have made contributions in all three of these areas.

In the wake of 9/11 in 2001, and the devastating hurricane that battered Florida in 2004, both brothers dug deep into their personal fortunes and donated large amounts of money to the disaster relief funds.

In 2005, the brothers' home city of New Orleans suffered some of the worst floods in living memory when Hurricane Katrina hit the city. Rather than simply give money to help victims of the disaster, the brothers sprang into action. They hired a plane, filled it with 30,000 pounds (13.6 mt) of relief supplies (including water, baby formula, diapers, and pillows) and arranged for the plane to be flown to Louisiana. Once there, the brothers helped to distribute the supplies to those who needed them most.

In 2010, both brothers raised money for victims of the Deepwater Horizon oil spill, which affected thousands of people's health and businessses in the Gulf of Mexico. Along with other celebrities, the brothers appeared in a television commercial urging people to donate money to victims of the disaster.

The Deepwater Horizon oil spill polluted miles of coastline in the Gulf of Mexico. The disaster damaged wildlife, people's health, and local businesses.

HELPING HANDS FOR HOSPITALS

The Manning brothers have a passion for children's charities and the welfare of children, so it is no surprise that both brothers have a long history of assisting children's hospitals.

Shortly after he started playing for the Colts, Peyton began to donate money to a local children's hospital, St. Vincent's in Indianapolis. Peyton also visited patients and hosted parties around the holidays, as

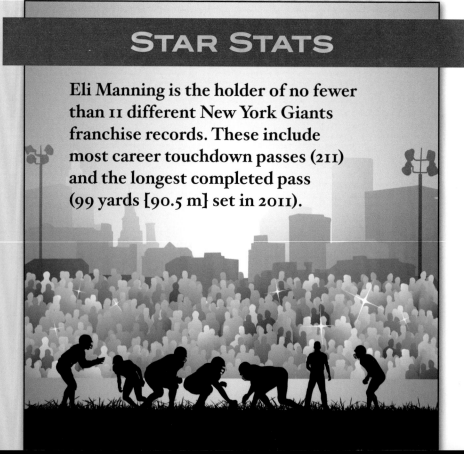

STAR STATS

Eli Manning is the holder of no fewer than 11 different New York Giants franchise records. These include most career touchdown passes (211) and the longest completed pass (99 yards [90.5 m] set in 2011).

Eli Manning autographs souvenirs while attending the 2009 BTIG Commissions for Charity Day. Over the years, BTIG, a global trading company, has raised more than $28 million for children's charititable organizations.

part of the PeyBack Foundation's True Heroes program. In 2007, to thank the sports star for his help and work at the hospital, St. Vincent's was renamed the Peyton Manning Children's Hospital.

In 2007, Eli made a trip to the University of Mississippi Medical Center's Blair E. Batson Hospital for Children, which inspired him to raise funds for the center. Eli made a five-year commitment to raise $2.5 million to fund the building of the Eli Manning Children's Clinic at the hospital. The clinic now provides health care services for up to 75,000 children a year.

If there is one thread that runs through all the charity work of the Manning brothers, it is a desire to see children better themselves. This might be by helping them to become better athletes or teaching them valuable leadership skills. The Manning brothers' charities also offer children programs that provide exciting and worthwhile alternatives to hanging out on the streets.

The one thing that ties all of the Manning's charitable initiatives together is education. The Mannings are passionate about encouraging children to widen their knowledge, improve their reading and writing, and learn new skills.

The Mannings' charities support after-school activities such as youth football coaching clubs.

Many of the charities funded by the PeyBack Foundation are linked to education. The brothers' favored charities often provide sports education through football coaching, or after-school reading or music clubs.

Peyton and Eli are both hugely committed to initiatives that help to give children, and teenagers in particular, the skills they need to make the most of their lives. The brothers have helped to fund scholarships that enable teenagers from disadvantaged backgrounds to attend college.

STAR STATS

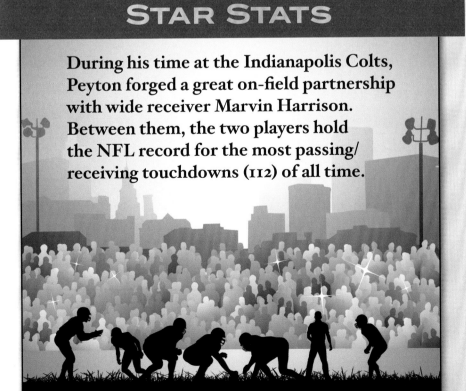

During his time at the Indianapolis Colts, Peyton forged a great on-field partnership with wide receiver Marvin Harrison. Between them, the two players hold the NFL record for the most passing/receiving touchdowns (112) of all time.

35

A College Education

Peyton and Eli Manning had a privileged childhood. They attended a private high school in Louisiana, and had their college fees paid for by their parents.

The brothers' achievements and experiences at college taught them that obtaining a college degree is a great way to get ahead in life.

Many parents cannot afford to pay for college, and instead look to scholarships to help fund their children's education. The scholarships help gifted students from disadvantaged backgrounds continue their education. Many colleges have their own scholarships, while some charities offer awards toward college costs.

In 2009, Peyton Manning launched the PeyBack Foundation Scholarship. Each year, one student at a high school involved in the PeyBack Classic event receives the Scholarship and is given $10,000-a-year toward the cost of college.

Winning the award is tough. To even be nominated for the award students must show they are involved in sports, contribute to their

community through charity or social work, and
have excellent exam results. The 2011 recipient
of the award, Jacob Slusher, captained his
high school football team, volunteered for
two different charities, and coached at his
local youth wrestling club!

Peyton Manning congratulates the 2013 PeyBack
Foundation Scholarship recipient, Matt Fitzpatrick,
at Heritage Christian School, Indianapolis.

READ WITH THE MANNINGS

As part of their commitment to encouraging children to be the best they can be, both Peyton and Eli Manning continually highlight the importance of being able to read.

Since 2009, both brothers have been vocal supporters of programs that encourage children to read more, both through charities funded by the PeyBack Foundation and their links with the Scholastic Book Club. This initiative is from the Scholastic book publishing company. It offers schools, parents,

STAR STATS

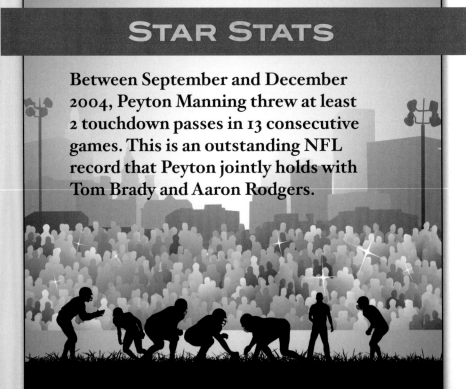

Between September and December 2004, Peyton Manning threw at least 2 touchdown passes in 13 consecutive games. This is an outstanding NFL record that Peyton jointly holds with Tom Brady and Aaron Rodgers.

and children the opportunity to buy new books each month far more cheaply than they could online or in bookstores. For every book children or parents buy, their school also earns points. The points can then be used to buy further discounted books for the school classrooms or libraries.

The partnership between the Manning brothers and Scholastic began in 2008, when Peyton and Eli joined forces with father Archie to write a children's book. Called *Family Huddle*, the book is based on the brothers' experiences of playing backyard football with their father while growing up in New Orleans.

Schoolchildren across the United States have been able to enjoy wonderful literature as a result of the the PeyBack Foundation and Scholastic Book Club's contributions to school libraries and classrooms.

HEALTHY CHOICES

As professional football players, Peyton and Eli Manning understand the importance of being physically active and leading a healthy life. The brothers have tried to use their knowledge to inspire children to lead healthier lives themselves.

Peyton is an active supporter of Project 18, a program established by St. Vincent Children's Hospital, Marsh Supermarkets, and Ball State University. The program encourages kids to be healthy and active, and also raises money to support weight management health care for overweight children and teenagers.

As part of Project 18, Peyton helped to create a child-friendly cookbook of healthy recipes for mealtime favorites. The recipes use healthy ingredients and cooking methods in order to encourage children to eat healthy and nutritious food rather than unhealthy, fast food.

Eli has also encouraged children to eat nutritious food and play more sports. For several years, the football star was a council member of the President's Council on Fitness, Sports, and Nutrition. This government body aims to motivate Americans to play more sports. Eli has regularly attended Council meetings and offered

Project 18 encourages children and young people to make positive food choices that will benefit their health and well-being.

his own ideas for ways in which to encourage children to lead healthier and more active lives.

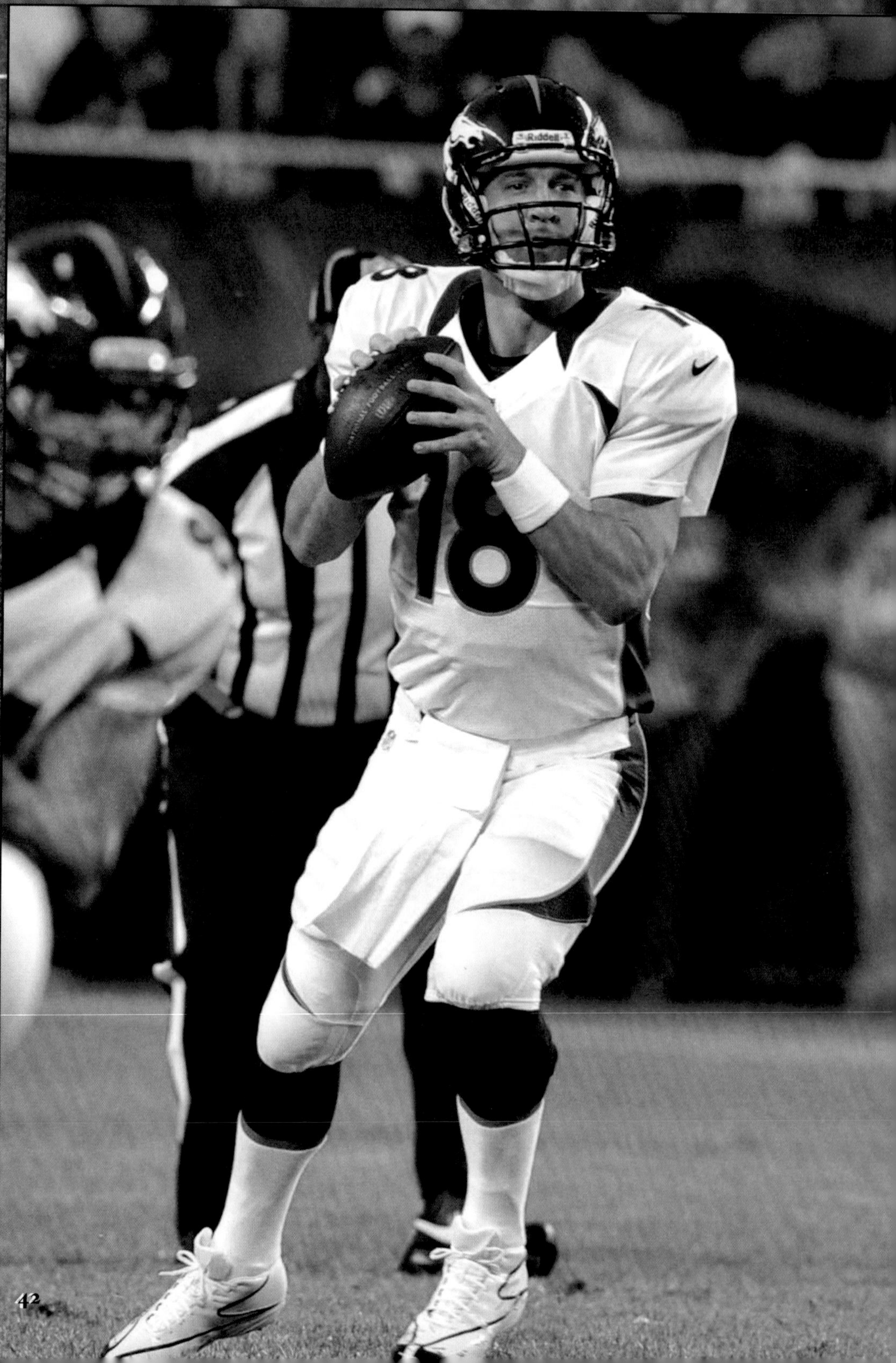

COMMUNITY CHAMPIONS

Many people believe that Peyton and Eli Manning are perfect role models. From an early age, the brothers have excelled in all aspects of their lives. They've worked hard for their success, and keep working hard to stay at the top of their game. They lead healthy lifestyles, help others less fortunate than themselves, and have raised millions of dollars for charity.

Both brothers have made an enormous impact on the football field, yet it is their off-field work for charity that may well be their greatest legacy. Long after they've hung up their football uniforms, Eli and Peyton will continue to work to better the lives of children in Louisiana, New York, Colorado, Indianapolis, and Mississippi. Football records can be broken, but the brothers' work in the community can never be undone. It is for this reason that the brothers will be remembered as sporting legends, but also as great people making a difference in their communities.

By the time they retire, Peyton and Eli Manning may well be considered as being among the greatest quarterbacks of all time. On all the records that count, the brothers are quite simply at the top of the charts.

1993: Peyton graduates from Isidore Newman School after leading his school team to a 34–5 win/loss record.

1994: Peyton starts college at the University of Tennessee and becomes the Tennessee Volunteers starting quarterback.

1998: Peyton graduates from the University of Tennessee, having become the Volunteers' all-time leading passer.

1998: Peyton joins the Indianapolis Colts, sets four NFL rookie records, and is named in the "All-Rookie" first team.

1999: Peyton launches the PeyBack Foundation.

2004: Eli is selected by New York Giants as the first pick of the 2004 NFL Draft.

2007: Peyton leads the Colts to victory in Super Bowl XLI, the final game of the 2006 season. He is named Super Bowl Most Valuable Player for the first time.

2008: Eli inspires New York Giants to a Super Bowl XLII win over the previously unbeaten New England Patriots. He is named Super Bowl Most Valuable Player.

2011: Peyton signs a new contract, reportedly worth $90 million, with the Indianapolis Colts.

2012: History repeats itself as Eli leads the Giants to a second Super Bowl victory over the New England Patriots, this time by 21 points to 17. Eli is named Most Valuable Player for a second time, joining an elite club of all-time greats who have won the award more than once.

2012: After being released by the Colts in March, Peyton signs to the Denver Broncos. After a relatively successful season, he is named NFL Comeback Player of the Year.

2013: Peyton is named in the line-up for the 2013 Pro Bowl—the twelfth time he has received the honor.

Kevin Durant
The National Basketball Association (NBA) and Olympic Team USA basketball star has raised money for various charities, including a $1 million donation to the America Red Cross to help victims of the Oklahoma City tornado in 2013.

Jeff Gordon
The leading National Association for Stock Car Auto Racing (NASCAR) driver works tirelessly to raise money for cancer charities.

Robert Griffin III
The pro football player began volunteering for a number of charities while still at college.

Mia Hamm
The leading soccer player's Mia Hamm Foundation raises money for families of children suffering from rare diseases.

Tony Hawk
The skateboarding legend's charity, The Tony Hawk Foundation, has provided more than $3.4 million to build 400 skate parks around the United States.

Derek Jeter
The New York Yankees shortstop started his Turn 2 Foundation to support youth programs across the United States.

Magic Johnson
The NBA legend founded the Magic Johnson Foundation in 1991 to fund a range of educational projects. Today, 250,000 young Americans benefit from its funded projects every year.

Kurt Warner
The former Super Bowl MVP's First Things First Foundation improves the lives of impoverished children.

Venus and Serena Williams
The record-breaking tennis players devote huge amounts of time to charity. They also champion equal rights for women.

also-rans Runners up, or people who didn't quite achieve their goals.

campaigns Work carried out with the aim of achieving a specific goal, such as raising money for charity.

communities Groups of people in one particular area or with common goals.

disadvantaged To have few opportunities in life.

fundraising The process of raising money for charity.

grants Money paid to help an individual or organization achieve a goal.

immortals People whose reputations live forever.

initiative A program or project.

legacy How a person is remembered after he or she has died.

nutritious Food that nourishes the body.

partnership Two or more people who have joined together to achieve something.

playoff A winner-takes-all game. In the playoffs, only the winners progress to play the next game. For the losers, their season is over.

privileged To have many advantages.

quarter A period of time in some sports games. There are four quarters in each game.

quarterbacks Players who are responsible for moving the ball around the field and passing to teammates.

retired To have stopped performing a role or a job.

"road" wins Wins at the stadium of the opponent.

role models People whose good behavior and attitude inspires others.

rookie A player in his or her first year as a professional athlete.

scholarship Money won by a student in order to study.

sponsorships Monies paid to an athlete or team by companies, in order to be associated with their success.

Super Bowl The game that ends the season and which decides the NFL football champions every year.

touchdown passes Passes that are caught in the other team's end zone, or run there by the catcher, thereby scoring a touchdown.

welfare Payments made by the government to poor people to ensure they have enough money to survive.

BOOKS

Christopher, Matt, and Stephanie Peters. *On the Field with... Peyton & Eli Manning*. New York, NY: Little, Brown Books, 2008.

Howse, Jennifer. *The Manning Brothers* (Remarkable People). New York, NY: Weigl Pub Inc, 2009.

Manning, Archie, Eli, and Peyton, and Jim Madsen. *Family Huddle*. New York, NY: Scholastic, 2009.

Marcovitz, Hal. *The Manning Brothers* (Superstars of Pro Football). Broomall, PA: Mason Crest Publishers, 2008.

Worthington, J. A. *The Mannings: Football's Famous Family*. Mankato, MN: Red Brick Learning, 2005.

WEBSITES

Due to the changing nature of Internet links, Rosen Publishing has developed an online list of Websites related to the subject of this book. This site is updated regularly. Please use this link to access the list:

http://www.rosenlinks.com/mad/mann